INSIDE THE NFL

NFC SOUTH

THE ATLANTA FALCONS
THE CAROLINA PANTHERS
THE NEW ORLEANS SAINTS
THE TAMPA BAY BUCCANEERS

BY K. C. KELLEY

The Child's World

Published in the United States of America by
The Child's World® • 1980 Lookout Drive
Mankato, MN 56003-1705

800-599-READ • www.childsworld.com

ACKNOWLEDGEMENTS

The Child's World®: Mary Berendes,
Publishing Director

The Design Lab: Kathleen Petelinsek,
Design; Gregory Lindholm, Page Production

Manuscript consulting and photo research
by Shoreline Publishing Group LLC.

Thanks to Jim Logan and Jim Gigliotti for their
help with this book.

PHOTOS

Cover: Front: Joe Robbins; back: Getty Images
Interior: AP/Wide World: 5, 8, 11, 12, 13, 14, 17,
18, 20, 23, 28, 31, 32; Getty Images: 6, 24, 27,
37; Joe Robbins: 26.

LIBRARY OF CONGRESS CATALOGING-IN-PUBLICATION DATA

Kelley, K. C.
  NFC South / by K.C. Kelley.
      p. cm. — (Inside the NFL)
  Includes bibliographical references and index.
  ISBN 978-1-59296-999-9
(library bound : alk. paper)
  1. National Football League—History—Juvenile
literature. 2. Football—United States—History—
Juvenile literature. I. Title. II. Series.
  GV955.5.N35K454 2008
  796.332'640973—dc22   2008010517

TABLE OF CONTENTS

TABLE OF CONTENTS

NFC SOUTH
INTRODUCTION

T he NFL underwent a major realignment in 2002 (meaning it changed the way its teams are organized) for the first time in more than 30 years. When the league decided to group its teams into eight divisions of four teams each that year, the National Football Conference (NFC) South was born.

The first year of the NFC South also marked the first year that one of its teams won a championship. The Atlanta Falcons, Carolina Panthers, New Orleans Saints, and Tampa Bay Buccaneers all existed before that, but it wasn't until the Buccaneers won **Super Bowl** XXXVII that year that any of them captured a title.

The teams in the NFC South are among the youngest in the 88-year-old NFL. Each one of them began as an **expansion team**. But even though they haven't been around as long as some other clubs, they all have rich histories filled with great teams and colorful players. Read on to learn more.

The natural geographic **rivalries**
in the NFC South mean that
there is lots of bone-crunching
action every time any of these
four teams get together.

CHAPTER ONE

THE ATLANTA FALCONS

N FL fans don't like to hear that their favorite team is in "rebuilding" mode. But that's just what the Atlanta Falcons found themselves in after a series of events in 2007 knocked them off a course they believed could take them to the Super Bowl. Still, Atlanta has overcome tough patches before and made it the NFL's biggest game—and Falcons' fans believe that they'll do it again.

The first time that the Falcons made it to the Super Bowl was in the 1998 season. Head coach Dan Reeves guided the squad to the big game only two years after the team suffered through a disastrous 3–13 season in 1996. Atlanta found itself in a similar position when it won only four games in 2007. It was one of the toughest seasons in club history.

That history began in 1966, when the Falcons first joined the NFL. They

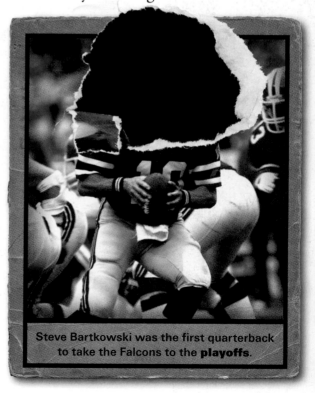

Steve Bartkowski was the first quarterback to take the Falcons to the **playoffs**.

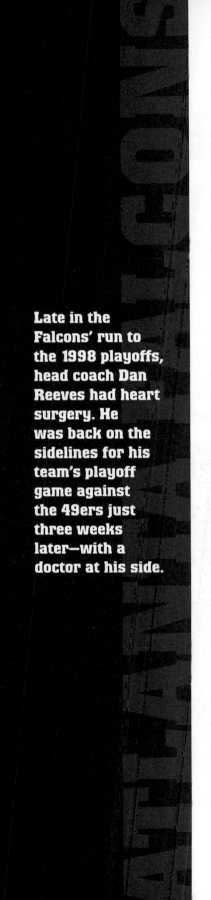

got off to a good start when they chose linebacker Tommy Nobis of the University of Texas with the first overall pick in the **draft** that year. Nobis had also been picked by the Houston Oilers, of the rival **American Football League** (AFL). American astronauts orbiting Earth begged Nobis to sign with Houston, home of the space program. However, Nobis went with Atlanta and gave the Falcons 11 great years.

Norb Hecker, the team's first coach, didn't last as long. The Falcons posted a 3–11 record their first year, then went 1–12–1 the next. After Atlanta lost its first three games of 1968, Hecker was replaced by former NFL quarterback Norm Van Brocklin. The Falcons finished with a 2–12 record.

Finally, in 1971, the team earned its first winning record, 7–6–1. Two years later, the Falcons went 9–5, but the 1970s mostly were a tough time for the team. Some good, though, came out of that decade. In 1975, Atlanta chose quarterback Steve Bartkowski of the University of California with the first pick overall in the draft.

With Bartkowski running the offense and the defense pounding opponents, the Falcons reached the **postseason** for the first time in 1978. They went 9–7 that year to finish second in the NFC West (their old division) and earn a **wild-card** playoff **berth.** They beat the Philadelphia Eagles in the first round of the playoffs but lost to the Dallas Cowboys in the next round.

Bartkowski's best year was 1980, when the Falcons won the West with a 12–4 record. They

Super Bowl XXXIII was a big disappointment to the Falcons. It was only after the game that they could reflect on the terrific season that got them there.

were nearly unstoppable. Bartkowski threw 31 touchdown passes, the best in the league, and running backs William Andrews and Lynn Cain combined for nearly 2,000 yards rushing.

Once again, though, the Cowboys ended their season. This time, it really hurt. The Falcons were ahead 24–10 going into the fourth quarter. Then, Dallas quarterback Danny White led his team to three touchdowns, the last one a 23-yard pass with 42 seconds left in the game. Final score: Cowboys 30, Falcons 27.

In the next 10 years, the Falcons had just one winning season (1982), and that season had only nine games because of a players' strike. A bright spot was Billy "White Shoes" Johnson, a dazzling kick returner and receiver. Big Gerald Riggs was a human battering ram at running back. It wasn't until 1990, when Jerry Glanville was hired as coach, that the team had better luck.

In 1991, with Deion "Prime Time" Sanders anchoring the defensive backfield, the Falcons swaggered to a 10–6 record. They looked ready to make a run through the playoffs after beating New Orleans in the first round. However, they lost to Washington in their next game. After back-to-back 6–10 seasons, Glanville was gone.

June Jones, a former Falcons backup quarterback, was hired as coach in 1994. The same year, the team acquired rocket-armed quarterback Jeff George in a trade from the Indianapolis Colts.

The Falcons posted a 7–9 record in George's first season. The next year, they went 9–7 behind Craig "Ironhead" Heyward's 1,083 rushing yards. They lost 37–20 to the Green Bay Packers in the first round of the playoffs.

Then came the disappointing three-win season in 1996, and soon Jones was replaced by former Denver Broncos coach Dan Reeves.

Two years later, the Falcons shocked the NFL by posting a **franchise**-best record of 14–2 and earning a trip to Super Bowl XXXIII against the Broncos—Reeves' old team. **Veteran** quarterback Chris Chandler and star running back Jamal

Anderson led Atlanta. But if the Falcons were the Cinderella team, the Broncos and quarterback John Elway were the clock striking midnight. Elway passed for 336 yards, and Denver's Terrell Davis ran for 102 more. Meanwhile, the Broncos' defense kept Chandler and Anderson from doing much damage. Denver won 34–19.

As they had since they started, the Falcons followed their good season with disappointing years. They posted losing records in each of their next three seasons.

And then an athletic, left-handed quarterback named Michael Vick arrived. The Falcons took the quarterback from Virginia Tech with the first pick overall in the 2001 draft. Vick had a cannon for an arm and speed that one player called "pretty close to cheetah."

In Vick's first full season as a starter in 2002, the Falcons won nine games and earned a wild-card playoff berth after finishing second in the new NFC South. Vick broke his leg in the preseason and missed most of the next year, and the Falcons won only five games. That cost Reeves his job.

Jim Mora Jr. was hired as coach in 2004 and reenergized a defense led by end Patrick Kerney. Kerney earned a **Pro Bowl** berth after making 13 sacks (tackling a quarterback behind the **line of scrimmage**). A healthy Vick took charge of the offense again, and Atlanta won 11 regular-season games and the NFC South championship.

The Falcons believed that group would take them back to the Super Bowl. But a couple of so-so

Running back Warrick Dunn is one of the NFL's best running backs—and one of its best citizens, too. In 2007, Dunn passed the 10,000-yard rushing mark and also earned the Home Depot NFL Neighborhood MVP award. That's given to the player who makes the most positive impact in a community.

A lot of experts thought Warrick Dunn was too small to make it in the NFL, but he's had a big-time career.

Wide receiver Roddy White was one of the few bright spots in a disappointing year for the Falcons in 2007.

seasons followed. And then came the difficult calendar year of 2007. First, Mora was fired just two seasons after his division championship. Kerney left for Seattle as a **free agent.** Vick was sent to jail for his role in an illegal dog-fighting operation. And new coach Bobby Petrino, who was highly successful in college at Louisville, couldn't turn the team around before he quit late in the season.

That left a lot of question marks heading into 2008. New coach Mike Smith, the former defensive coordinator of the Jacksonville Jaguars, was left to find the answers.

CHAPTER TWO
THE CAROLINA PANTHERS

R ight from the start, the Carolina Panthers have been on the fast track to success. Beginning with their first season in 1995, they experienced winning at a rate previously unheard of for an NFL expansion team. And although they have yet to experience the NFL's ultimate prize—a Super Bowl championship—they have come tantalizingly close.

The Panthers began play as a member of the NFC West in 1995. It was quickly apparent that, under first-time head coach Dom Capers, the Panthers were no ordinary expansion team. In fact, somebody forgot to tell the Panthers that expansion teams don't win much in their first season, because they won often. In their first year, they had a 7–9 record. That set a record for wins by a first-year expansion club.

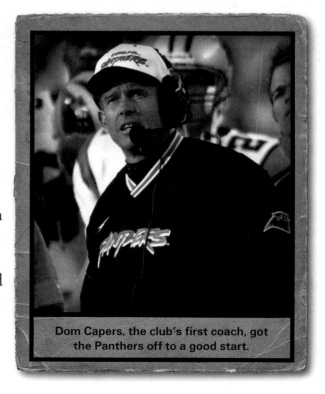

Dom Capers, the club's first coach, got the Panthers off to a good start.

**Quarterback Kerry Collins
throws a pass during the
Panthers' stunning upset of
the 49ers in 1995.**

The wins came on the field, but they started with the hard work
done by the team's owners and management long before any player
put on his uniform.

When the NFL announced in 1993 that Carolina would be
the league's 29th franchise, owner Jerry Richardson got to work.
Richardson was a former wide receiver for the Colts who had become
a successful restaurant company owner. He hired experienced football
men to run the club, and they made smart moves. First, they hired
Dom Capers, who had been the Pittsburgh Steelers' defensive
coordinator, as head coach. Then they picked a team.

Mike McCormack retired as the Panthers' club president in 1997. That ended his 46-year career as an NFL player, coach, and executive.

Earlier expansion teams usually got players other clubs didn't want. The Panthers avoided that by signing veteran free agents. Linebackers Carlton Bailey, Lamar Lathon, and Sam Mills were signed that way. Receiver Willie Green and running back Derrick Moore also helped the team right away.

Carolina used its three first-round draft picks wisely. Quarterback Kerry Collins, tackle Blake Brockermeyer, and cornerback Tyrone Poole all started and played well.

The mix of veterans and **rookies** worked like magic. Carolina's seven victories in its first year included a shocking 13–7 upset of the 49ers—the team that had won Super Bowl XXIX in the 1994 season—in a game at San Francisco. It was the first time that an expansion team ever had beat a reigning Super Bowl champion, and it was part of a remarkable four-game winning streak.

The Panthers soon proved that their first-year performance was no fluke, however, because what they did in their second year was simply amazing. On its way to a 12–4 record during the regular season, Carolina beat the powerful 49ers twice. And when the Panthers beat Pittsburgh 18–14 on the final weekend of the season, the two wins over San Francisco gave them the tiebreaker edge with the 49ers. Carolina was a division champ in only its second season.

Linebacker Kevin Greene led the league that season with 14.5 sacks. The defense was second in the NFL in fewest points allowed—only 218 in 16 games. On offense, Collins showed signs of greatness. Running back Anthony Johnson ran for 1,120 yards. Kicker John Kasay had a league-high 37 field goals.

In the first round of the playoffs, the Panthers beat the defending Super Bowl champion Cowboys, 26–17. Brett Favre and the Packers ended the Panthers' season in the NFC Championship Game, 30–13. Carolina's **blitzing** was ineffective, and the Packers rushed for a surprisingly easy 201 yards. Still, seven Carolina players were named to the NFC Pro Bowl team, Capers was coach of the year, and it looked like the Panthers would be a powerhouse team for years to come.

As things turned out, it took several seasons (and a couple of coaching changes) for Carolina to build on its early success. In 1997, Collins broke his jaw in a preseason game against the Denver Broncos and had a tough year, throwing 21 **interceptions** with just 11 touchdowns. The Panthers wobbled to a 7–9 record.

The next year was worse. Four games into the season, Collins was **released** by the team. Steve Beuerlein stepped in as quarterback, but the Panthers never got in gear and finished 4–12. Capers was fired and replaced by George Seifert. Seifert had a record of success. He had won two Super Bowls and 108 games in his eight years as coach of the 49ers.

In Seifert's first year, 1999, the Panthers were better, but they still finished 8–8. The highlight of the season was the passing game. Beuerlein threw for 4,436 yards and 36 touchdowns, most of them

Does the team's helmet logo look familiar? Check out a map! The panther head is in the shape of North and South Carolina.

Quarterback Steve Beuerlein had a huge season in 1999, when he set club records for passing yards (4,436) and touchdown passes (36).

to wide receivers Muhsin Muhammad and Patrick Jeffers and tight end Wesley Walls.

After a 7–9 season in 2000, the Panthers fell apart in 2001. With 2000 **Heisman Trophy** winner Chris Weinke at quarterback, Carolina won just one game. It wasn't all Weinke's fault. Although the offense was the second worst in the league, the defense ranked dead last. Seifert was let go.

Quarterback Jake Delhomme and the Panthers nearly made it to the top of the NFL in 2003. They lost a heartbreaking game to the Patriots in the Super Bowl.

For 2002, John Fox, defensive coordinator for the New York Giants the previous five seasons, was hired as coach. With a **roster** of young players sprinkled with veterans, Fox's team showed immediate, and dramatic, improvement. Playing in the newly formed NFC South, the Panthers won their first three games under their new leader. They finished the 2002 season with a 7–9 record.

The promise of that season was fulfilled the next year. Jake Delhomme, a free-agent signee from New Orleans, took over as quarterback and passed for 3,219 yards and Fox's defense, featuring young end Julius Peppers, was one of the best in the league. Carolina won 11 games and cruised to the NFC South championship.

After beating Dallas 29–10 in the opening round of the playoffs, the visiting Panthers stunned St. Louis in the divisional round, winning 29–23 on Delhomme's 69-yard touchdown strike to Steve Smith on the first play of the second overtime. For the second time in its brief history, Carolina was in the NFC title game. And this time, the Panthers won it. They reached their first Super Bowl by upsetting host Philadelphia 14–3.

Though Super Bowl XXXVIII resulted in a heartbreaking, 32–29 loss to New England, the 2003 season was an unqualified success. The Panthers haven't been back to the Super Bowl since then, but they did come close in 2005. An 11-win season earned them a wild-card playoff berth that year. Then Carolina beat the New York Giants and the Chicago Bears in the playoffs before falling to the Seattle Seahawks on the road in the NFC Championship Game.

Fox came to Carolina with a reputation as a defensive mastermind. And the Panthers' defense has been successful under his leadership. But he also has built an excellent offense around players such as Delhomme, Smith, and running backs DeShaun Foster and DeAngelo Williams.

CHAPTER THREE

THE NEW ORLEANS SAINTS

F ew sports franchises ever have meant as much to their city as the Saints have to New Orleans and to the surrounding area in recent years. The town's football team has become a symbol of hope and rebirth to an area that was devastated by Hurricane Katrina in 2005.

Katrina hit the Gulf Coast of the United States in August that year. When the levees protecting New Orleans from river waters broke, the city found itself underwater. The Louisiana Superdome, the home of the Saints, was converted into a makeshift shelter for many of the area's residents who were forced to leave their homes. The Superdome itself suffered considerable damage, too. The NFL had to move the Saints' games in 2005 to Baton Rouge, Louisiana, and San Antonio, Texas. The turmoil led to a three-win season for the Saints.

Drew Brees has helped turn the Saints' offense into one of the league's best.

Then, as the city began to rebuild, so did the Saints. The club hired offensive wizard Sean Payton as its new head coach in 2006. Free-agent Drew Brees was brought in as quarterback. Exciting running back Reggie Bush joined the team as the second overall pick of the draft.

And, remarkably, the team returned to the Superdome in time for the 2006 home opener. The Saints' first game back in the stadium was a Monday-night contest against the division-rival Falcons. A rowdy home crowd cheered the team on to a 23–3 victory.

That was only the beginning. Brees went on to pass for a club-record 4,418 yards, Bush gained 1,307 yards from scrimmage, and the Saints won 10 games and the NFC South title.

Then the team beat the Eagles for just its second playoff win ever. The club's Super Bowl dreams ended with a loss to the Bears in the NFC Championship Game, but its success helped reenergize the entire region.

Saints' players reached out to the community in whatever way possible, too. It was only fitting that they stood by their fans in their tough times. After all, those same fans stood by the Saints through a lot of difficult seasons before the team tasted success.

Amazingly, the Saints had to wait 20 years before they enjoyed their first winning season. New Orleans was granted an NFL expansion franchise on All Saints' Day (November 1) in 1966. The team began play in the 1967 season.

At the time, the only way to build a team was through veterans nearing the end of their careers and youngsters just coming out of college. There was no such thing as true free agency, where players in the prime of their careers could play out a contract with one team and sign with anyone else. Instead, the players available were not wanted by their old teams, and few were good enough to build a team around. The Saints found this out when they signed two former Green Bay Packers running backs: future Hall of Famer Paul Hornung and one-time great Jim Taylor.

Unfortunately for the Saints, Hornung retired before training camp and Taylor played just one season, then retired as well.

One player who did help the team was quarterback Billy Kilmer, who put up good numbers even if the Saints didn't win much. Kilmer eventually was traded to the Washington Redskins, but not before he got to see one of the greatest plays in Saints' history. In 1970, Tom Dempsey kicked an NFL-record, 63-yard field goal on the final play to beat the Detroit Lions, 19–17.

Such great moments were rare, though. Not even great players such as quarterback Archie Manning, the second player taken in the 1971 draft, could help. Manning was a wizard with the football, but he was not surrounded with a lot of talented teammates. Through the years, the Saints drafted some good players—including running backs Chuck Muncie and George Rogers and wide receiver Wes Chandler—but not enough of them.

Archie Manning, who played for New Orleans from 1971 to 1982, was the first of the famous Manning NFL quarterbacks. He is the father of the Indianapolis Colts' Peyton Manning and the New York Giants' Eli Manning.

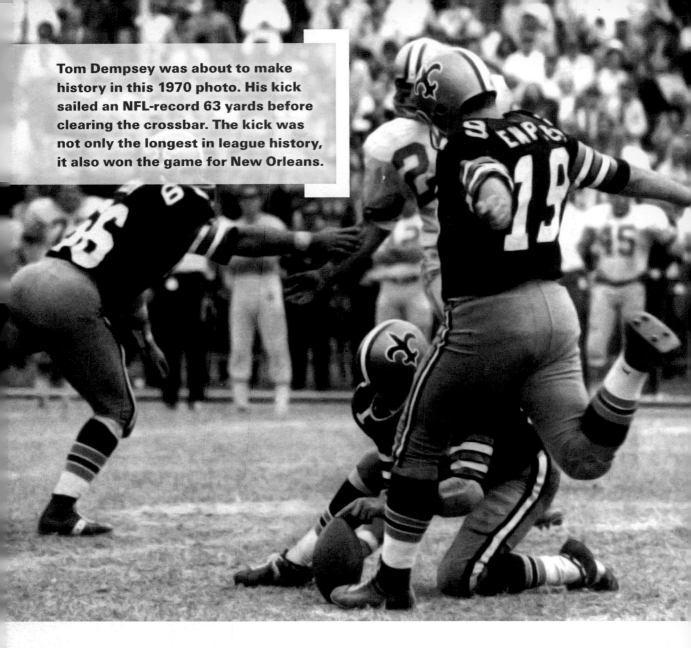

Tom Dempsey was about to make history in this 1970 photo. His kick sailed an NFL-record 63 yards before clearing the crossbar. The kick was not only the longest in league history, it also won the game for New Orleans.

The club went through a string of coaches with no better luck. Not even a new stadium, the Louisiana Superdome, helped. The Saints made it their home in 1975 and won only two games that year.

What is surely the team's low point came in 1980. New Orleans was coming off an 8–8 season, and hopes were high. But the Saints stumbled to a 1–15 season. Fans started coming to games with paper bags over their heads and calling the team the "'Aints."

In 1987, Louisiana native Bobby Hebert (pronounced AY-bear) marched the Saints into the playoffs.

The team's luck began to change in 1985. New owner Tom Benson hired respected football man Jim Finks as **general manager.** Finks hired Jim Mora, who had been a winner in the **United States Football League** (USFL), as head coach. In Mora's first season, 1986, the Saints finished at 7–9. Running back Rueben Mayes gained 1,353 yards and was named the league's rookie of the year.

Finally, in 1987, the Saints were winners. Twenty years after the birth of the franchise, New Orleans went 12–3. The fans loved quarterback Bobby Hebert (AY-bear), a Louisiana native from Baton Rouge. The season ended with a 44–10 loss to the Vikings in the playoffs.

Under Mora, the Saints were competitive and reached the playoffs in 1990, 1991, and 1992. The high point came in 1992, when the defense led the NFL in fewest points allowed (202) and in sacks (57) to finish with a 12–4 record. The Saints lost to the Eagles in the first round of playoffs.

The Mora era ended in 1996. Mike Ditka, who had led the Chicago Bears to victory in Super Bowl XX, eventually was hired as head coach. After consecutive 6–10 seasons, Ditka shocked the football world. He announced that he would trade all the Saints' draft picks for the fifth overall pick. With it, he chose Heisman Trophy winner Ricky Williams of Texas. Unfortunately, Williams struggled to adjust to the NFL and the Saints finished 3–13 in 1999. Ditka was fired.

In 2000, former Saints assistant coach and defensive coordinator Jim Haslett was hired as head coach. He made an immediate impact. He led the team to its second division title and, 33 years after it was founded, its first playoff victory. New Orleans won a 31–28 nail-biter over the defending Super Bowl champion St. Louis Rams. Although the Saints lost to the Vikings in the next round, the message was clear: The New Orleans Saints were winners.

With a tough, stingy defense and young offensive standouts such as running back Deuce McAllister and receiver Donte' Stallworth, the Saints appeared primed for a march into the Super Bowl.

It didn't work out that way. The team was almost always competitive, but it did not make the playoffs again until 2006. Then the Saints took

**Electrifying running back
Reggie Bush is a skilled
rushing and receiving threat.**

a step back in '07, narrowly missing a return trip to the postseason.
Still, the team came on strong that year after a bad beginning. Seven
wins after an 0–4 start gave the Saints hope for the future—hope that
the whole city shares.

CHAPTER FOUR
THE TAMPA BAY BUCCANEERS

T he history of the Tampa Bay Buccaneers' franchise has been filled with the highest of highs and the lowest of lows. From a winless season in the franchise's first year in 1976, to a Super Bowl championship in 2002, Buccaneers' fans have ridden a roller coaster of emotions. There have been very good times and very bad times, and just about everything in between!

Consider the club's most recent history. In 2007, the Buccaneers went 10–6 during the regular season and won the NFC South for the third time since the division was formed in 2002. That was a dramatic turnaround from a four-win, last-place finish in 2006. Of course, that last-place showing in '06 came after a division championship in '05— which came, as you might have guessed, after a last-place finish in '04. It's been a dizzying ride!

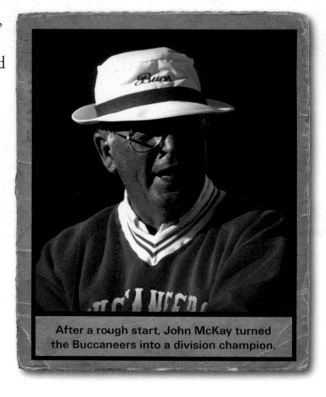

After a rough start, John McKay turned the Buccaneers into a division champion.

Quarterback Doug Williams
and the Buccaneers were
the surprise of the NFL in
1979, when they reached the
conference title game.

Still, few teams can appreciate the ride to the top quite as much
as the Buccaneers, considering where they began. No NFL team ever
had a more humbling start.

Tampa Bay began its existence as an expansion team in 1976,
and the Buccaneers lost every game. Then they dropped their first
12 games of 1977, too. But head coach John McKay, who had won
four national championships at the University of Southern California

(USC), had a plan for making the Buccaneers title contenders. He stuck with that plan even in the team's darkest hours.

That first Tampa Bay team, which played in the AFC West before moving to the NFC Central the next season, had one true star: defensive end Lee Roy Selmon. The Buccaneers made Selmon their number one draft pick, and he went on to earn a place in the Pro Football Hall of Fame. But first, he and the rest of the Buccaneers had to survive that grueling inaugural season.

It wasn't easy. The offense scored more than 20 points only once, and the defense had trouble stopping anybody. McKay, when asked what he thought of the team's execution, jokingly replied, "I'm in favor of it."

The losing streak finally ended in the next-to-last game in 1977. The Buccaneers' defense tied an NFL record (since broken) by returning three interceptions for touchdowns in a 33–14 victory over the Saints. For good measure, Tampa Bay won the following week, too, beating the St. Louis Cardinals 17–7.

The Buccaneers were the talk of the NFL when they won their first five games in 1979. Led by quarterback Doug Williams and former USC tailback Ricky Bell, Tampa Bay made it to the NFC title game against the Los Angeles Rams. The offense, however, couldn't get going and the Rams won, 9–0.

The Buccaneers made the playoffs in 1981 and 1982, then the dark times returned. After two more frustrating years, McKay retired following the

1984 season. In the 13 seasons from 1983 to 1995, the Buccaneers averaged 11 losses and won more than six games just once.

In 1995, the team got new ownership and, it seems, a fresh start. Tony Dungy was brought in to coach the Buccaneers in 1996. They started slow, but finished strong to post a 6–10 record.

The next year Tampa Bay used a ferocious defense and a solid running game to post its first winning record (10–6) in 16 years. The defense revolved around tackle Warren Sapp, who was as talkative as he was dominating. The offense was powered by the running team of Warrick Dunn and Mike Alstott. Dunn, the league's offensive rookie of the year, darted and slashed his way to 978 yards rushing. Alstott was a bulldozer in shoulder pads who piled up 665 yards.

The high point of the Dungy era came in 1999, when the Buccaneers posted a franchise-best 11–5 record and advanced to the NFC Championship Game against the Rams. In a brutal defensive struggle, Tampa Bay fell short, 11–6. Sapp was named the league's defensive player of the year.

After the 2001 season, fiery Jon Gruden replaced the mild-mannered Tony Dungy. The Buccaneers paid a steep price to pry Gruden away from the Oakland Raiders. They gave Oakland $8 million and four high draft choices. Gruden showed he was worth it.

In the 2002 regular season, Tampa Bay posted a 12–4 record and roared through the playoffs to earn its first trip to the Super Bowl. The opponent: Gruden's old team, the Raiders.

In 2007, the Buccaneers' Michael Spurlock returned a kickoff 90 yards for a touchdown against Atlanta. How unusual was that? Spurlock's runback came on the 1,865th kickoff return in Tampa Bay history—and it was the first one for a touchdown.

In their 27th season in 2002, the Buccaneers finally won a championship. Quarterback Brad Johnson (14) and safety John Lynch (47) enjoy the celebratory parade.

It looked like a classic matchup. The Raiders, behind the passing of league MVP Rich Gannon, had the NFL's number-one offense. The Buccaneers boasted the number-one defense. Something had to give. It was the Raiders.

Tampa Bay's defense made Gannon look like a rookie. The Buccaneers intercepted him five times. They set a Super Bowl record by running back three of those thefts for touchdowns. Safety Dexter Jackson picked off two passes and was named the game's MVP. Gannon also was sacked five times, and the Raiders managed just 62 yards in total offense in the first half. On offense, Buccaneers quarterback Brad Johnson completed 18 of 34 passes for 215 yards and two touchdowns. Receiver Keenan McCardell caught two

Quarterback Jeff Garcia turned in a Pro Bowl effort as up-and-down Tampa Bay was on the upswing again in 2007.

touchdown passes. Running back Michael Pittman rushed for 124 yards. Five minutes into the third quarter the Buccaneers led, 34–3.

The Raiders tried to make a game of it, but the Buccaneers' defense was just too much. Sapp and defensive lineman Simeon Rice wreaked havoc in the middle. Linebackers Derrick Brooks and Shelton Quarles stuffed both run and pass. Cornerback Dwight Smith returned two interceptions for touchdowns. Cornerback Brian Kelly had a team-high eight tackles and smothered Raiders receivers Tim Brown and Jerry Rice.

Final score: 48–21. For the Buccaneers, it was heaven. For the rest of the NFL, it meant trouble.

"We're young, we're good, we're going to have to be [reckoned] with a long time," said Smith.

It sure seemed that way at the time. But the following years did not quite go as Smith envisioned. The defense remained one of the league's best for several seasons, with Brooks and cornerback Ronde Barber leading the way. But the offense could not keep up, and Tampa Bay dropped off to seven wins the season after its Super Bowl victory, then, surprisingly, to only five wins in 2004.

Even the division championship in 2005 seemed only like an **aberration** when the Buccaneers slipped back to the bottom of the NFC South in '06. For the first time in many years, the defense no longer seemed to strike fear into Tampa Bay opponents. That unit fell to 17th in the league in total defense. The offense was inconsistent.

But Gruden guided the team back to the top of the division in 2007. Veteran Jeff Garcia was signed as a free agent to play quarterback and run Gruden's version of the **West Coast Offense.** Garcia quickly developed a **rapport** with big-play wide receiver Joey Galloway and made the Pro Bowl that season. The defense soared to number two in the league.

The Buccaneers clinched the division title with a 37–3 romp over the Falcons with two weeks still to play in the regular season. Eventually, the year ended with a disappointing loss to the Giants in the opening round of the playoffs.

Now Tampa Bay fans hope that the up-and-down elevator ride that they have been on will remain near the top for a while.

TIME LINE

1966
Atlanta Falcons join the NFL as an expansion team

1967
New Orleans Saints begin their first season as an expansion team

1971
Falcons post first their winning record, going 7–6–1

1960

1970

1980

1976
Tampa Bay Buccaneers begin play as an expansion team

1979
Buccaneers reach the NFC Championship Game in just their fourth season, but lose to the Los Angeles Rams

1987
Saints have first winning season, going 12–3

1995
Carolina Panthers begin first season as an expansion team

1996
Panthers reach NFC Championship Game in their second year, but their Super Bowl hopes are dashed by the Green Bay Packers

1998
Falcons reach Super Bowl XXXIII, lose to the Denver Broncos

1999
Buccaneers reach NFC Championship Game, but lose a close decision to the St. Louis Rams

1990   **2000**   **2010**

2002
Tampa Bay wins its first championship, beating the Oakland Raiders in Super Bowl XXXVII

2006
New Orleans reaches the NFC Championship Game for the first time, but loses to Chicago

STAT STUFF

TEAM RECORDS (THROUGH 2007)

Team	All-time Record	Number of Titles (Most Recent)	Number of Times in Playoffs	Top Coach (Wins)
Atlanta	262–386–6	0	8	Dan Reeves (52)
Carolina	103–114–0	0	3	John Fox (56)
New Orleans	256–373–5	0	6	Jim Mora (93)
Tampa Bay	202–312–1	1 (2002)	10	Tony Dungy (56)

NFC SOUTH CAREER LEADERS (THROUGH 2007)

Category	Name (Years With Team)	Total
Atlanta		
Rushing yards	Gerald Riggs (1982–88)	6,631
Passing yards	Steve Bartkowski (1975–1985)	23,468
Touchdown passes	Steve Bartkowski (1975–1985)	154
Receptions	Terance Mathis (1994–2001)	573
Touchdowns	Terance Mathis (1994–2001)	57
Scoring	Morten Andersen (1995–2000, 2006–07)	806
Carolina		
Rushing yards	DeShaun Foster (2003–07)	3,336
Passing yards	Jake Delhomme (2003–07)	13,957
Touchdown passes	Jake Delhomme (2003–07)	97
Receptions	Muhsin Muhammad (1996–2004)	578
Touchdowns	Steve Smith (2001–07)	45
Scoring	John Kasay (1995–2007)	1,162
New Orleans		
Rushing yards	Deuce McAllister (2001–07)	5,678
Passing yards	Archie Manning (1971–1982)	21,734
Touchdown passes	Aaron Brooks (2000–05)	120
Receptions	Eric Martin (1985–1993)	532
Touchdowns	Dalton Hilliard (1986–1993)	53
Scoring	Morten Andersen (1982–1994)	1,318
Tampa Bay		
Rushing yards	James Wilder (1981–89)	5,957
Passing yards	Vinny Testaverde (1987–1992)	14,820
Touchdown passes	Vinny Testaverde (1987–1992)	77
Receptions	James Wilder (1981–89)	430
Touchdowns	Mike Alstott (1996–2007)	71
Scoring	Martin Gramatica (1999–2004)	592

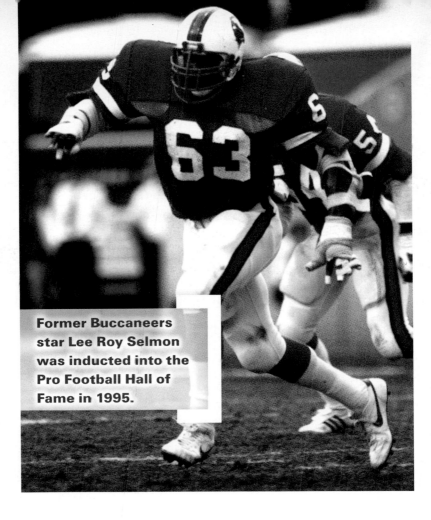

Former Buccaneers star Lee Roy Selmon was inducted into the Pro Football Hall of Fame in 1995.

MEMBERS OF THE PRO FOOTBALL HALL OF FAME

Player	Position	Date Inducted
Atlanta		
Eric Dickerson	Running Back	1999
Tommy McDonald	Wide Receiver	1998
Carolina		
Reggie White	Defensive End	2006
New Orleans		
Doug Atkins	Defensive End	1982
Earl Campbell	Running Back	1991
Jim Finks	General Manager	1995
Hank Stram	Coach	2003
Jim Taylor	Fullback	1976
Tampa Bay		
Lee Roy Selmon	Linebacker	1995
Steve Young	Quarterback	2005

GLOSSARY

aberration—out of the ordinary; unusual

American Football League—begun in 1960 as a rival to the NFL

berth—a space (in this case, a space in the playoffs)

blitzing—rushing the quarterback by the linebackers or defensive backs

draft—held each April, this is when NFL teams choose college players to join their teams; teams with the worst records the prior year choose first, but draft picks can be traded to move a team's draft order

expansion team—a new franchise that starts from scratch

franchise—more than just the team, it is the entire organization that is a member of a professional sports league

free agent—players who sign with any team they can contract with

general manager—the executive who runs the team for the owner

Heisman Trophy—the yearly award given to the best college football player

interceptions—passes caught by defensive players

line of scrimmage—an imaginary line that goes from sideline to sideline at the spot where each play begins

playoffs—after the regular schedule, these are the games played to determine the champion

postseason—the period in which the playoffs are held

Pro Bowl—the NFL's all-star game

rapport—a good relationship

released—when a player is let go by his team

rivalries—when people (or teams) compete for the same goal

rookies—athletes who are in their first season as a professional

roster—a list of a team's players

Super Bowl— the NFL's yearly championship game, played in late January or early February at a different stadium each year

United States Football League—a rival league formed in 1982

veteran—a player who is experienced from many seasons in the league

West Coast Offense—any of a number of offensive systems that rely on short, high-percentage passes and timing routes between the quarterback and his receivers

wild card—a team that makes the playoffs without winning a division title

FIND OUT MORE

Books

Goodman, Michael E. *The History of the Atlanta Falcons.* Mankato, Minn.: Creative Education, 2005.

Goodman, Michael E. *The History of the Tampa Bay Buccaneers.* Mankato, Minn.: Creative Education, 2005.

Ladewski, Paul. *National Football League Superstars 2007.* New York: Scholastic, 2007.

Marini, Matt. *Football Top 10.* New York: DK Publishing, 2002.

Stewart, Mark. *The Carolina Panthers.* Chicago: Norwood House Press, 2007.

Stewart, Mark. *The New Orleans Saints.* Chicago: Norwood House Press, 2007.

On the Web

Visit our Web site for lots of links about the NFC South: *http://www.childsworld.com/links*

Note to Parents, Teachers, and Librarians: We routinely verify our Web links to make sure they are safe, active sites—so encourage your readers to check them out!

INDEX